INTROS, ENDINGS & TURNAROUNDS FOR UKULELE

BY LIL' REV

Editorial Assistance by Will Branch

To access video visit:
www.halleonard.com/mylibrary

8535-4572-6061-1465

ISBN: 978-1-4950-5665-9

HAL•LEONARD®

Copyright © 2018 by HAL LEONARD LLC
International Copyright Secured   All Rights Reserved

Visit Hal Leonard Online at
www.halleonard.com

Contact Us:
Hal Leonard
7777 West Bluemound Road
Milwaukee, WI 53213
Email: info@halleonard.com

In Europe contact:
Hal Leonard Europe Limited
Distribution Centre, Newmarket Road
Bury St Edmunds, Suffolk, IP33 3YB
Email: info@halleonardeurope.com

In Australia contact:
Hal Leonard Australia Pty. Ltd.
4 Lentara Court
Cheltenham, Victoria, 3192 Australia
Email: info@halleonard.com.au

CONTENTS

INTRODUCTION

The late cowboy philosopher Will Rogers was once quoted as saying, "The ukulele had this advantage: even a trained professional couldn't tell whether someone was just goofing off or really knew what they were doing."

In some ways I agree with Mr. Rogers. Though the overall ability of people to perform intricate melodic and rhythmic material on the ukulele has skyrocketed, there is still a huge void left to be filled with regards to intros and endings. Setting up a song's delivery, as well as its ending, in an interesting and enticing manner has fallen from vogue. Many club strummers may be content to begin a song on its tonic (starting chord) and then launch into the song without much fanfare or pretext.

Likewise, ukulele song leaders the world over have put little emphasis on ending a song with anything more than a crash-bang-boom, I-chord finale. But many legends, from Louis Armstrong to Chuck Berry, have left us with a full palette of ways to end a song with grace, grit, and humor. That's why I have decided to dedicate a whole book to the lost art of intros and endings.

While the sole purpose of every introduction is to open the door to its subsequent song, intros (like endings) can run the gamut from sultry and sweet to raucous and rollicking. After almost 100 years of recorded music history, we can look back and see that these key musical devices can be as memorable as the greatest pop song hook or as obnoxious as a "Shave and a Haircut" bluegrass ending.

Should you endeavor to study the lost art of intros and endings with the kind of tenacity that has driven guitarists like Lonnie Johnson, Eddie Lang, or Charlie Christian, here's what you'll discover:

- Improved understanding of chord families and sequences

- How intros and endings can be easily transposed to your favorite keys

- New and exciting ways to play inverted (or moveable) chord forms

- An encouraging way to look beyond the confines of first-position strumming

- How to turn almost any intro into an ending by adding a V chord

- How a few snazzy chords added to the front or back end of a song can go a long way to improving an arrangement

Ukefully,
Lil' Rev

www.lilrev.com

HOW TO USE THIS BOOK

This book is designed to be a collection of examples. Some may endeavor to study it from start to finish, and others may want to jump around based on the type of music that they are currently arranging. Perhaps it'd be best to think of this as a free-flowing compendium of ideas. For example, if you are working on an arrangement of "On the Sunny Side of the Street," then you might want to try out the Gus Kahn (Broadway Era) Intro to see if that suits the tune. Or perhaps you've cemented the lyrics and chords to "Sweet Home Chicago," and you want to master a classic blues turnaround. Then you'd go right to the appropriate section of this book that best serves your current musical taste.

Rather than lumping together the similar examples, I have staggered them for the sake of variety. Stylistically, these gems range from Tin Pan Alley, blues, and ragtime to jazz, bluegrass, and rock, though many of these are interchangeable and can be used across a number of different genres.

For each example, I'll offer you a couple of options from which to choose, though my hope is that you'll begin to assimilate each of these into a wide variety of different keys. Along these lines, I would suggest you begin to study the concept of *transposing*—i.e., taking musical pieces that are presented in a specific key, and being able to try them out in another, often more suitable key. Typically, if we are talking about songs with vocals, the most specific reason for being able to transpose is to create an arrangement that is suitable to the singer's voice. However, instrumental pieces beg for intros and endings with the same authority as vocal tunes and thus, everyone has at least a couple of favorite keys they like to play in. It's best to be flexible as you grow to become a great musician.

ABOUT THE VIDEO

Each chapter in the book includes a video lesson, so you can see and hear the material being taught. To access all of the videos that accompany this book, simply visit **www.halleonard.com/mylibrary** and enter the code found on page 1.

Tips

Keep the following in mind as you work through the book:

- Watch each video example to capture the right strum feel.

- Adding tremolo to the last chord in an intro (on the V chord) can enhance its appeal.

- Though the book often shows the examples in various keys, the videos typically demonstrate only one key.

NOTATION

Regarding the notation, the following system is used throughout the book.

For strumming examples, rhythm slashes ⁄ are used. Each slash is equal to a strum or stroke. For example: ⁄⁄ would be equal to two strokes.

For single-note examples, rhythm tab will be used.

LIL' REV'S ALL-PURPOSE INTRO AND ENDING

The first intro we'll tackle is one of the easiest in the book. Likewise, it's also the most versatile. It has its origins in doo-wop and blues, but time and time again, it's proven to be a real workhorse even amidst other styles of music like pop, rock, and early jazz. I play this with all downstrokes.

How to Set Up an Intro

An intro can create a great effect as an opening to a song. It's a little kernel of pizzazz that's waiting to be presented all by itself. One way that you can give the intro the respect it deserves is to add a breath or hesitation right after the intro, before launching into the actual song. This will create some suspense, drama, and a sense of anticipation. By taking a breath, I mean the equivalent of a "2-3-4" count. Since you'll often be striking a V chord for just one beat, adding this count after an intro gives it a little room to breathe before you launch into the song. It's a very classy way to start it off!

Let's begin with the Lil' Rev intro in C and F:

Key of C:

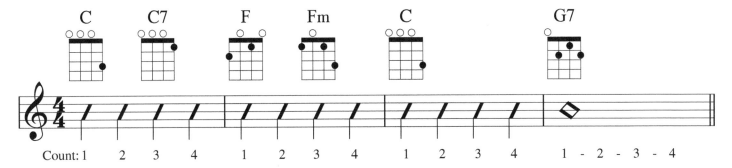

Key of F:

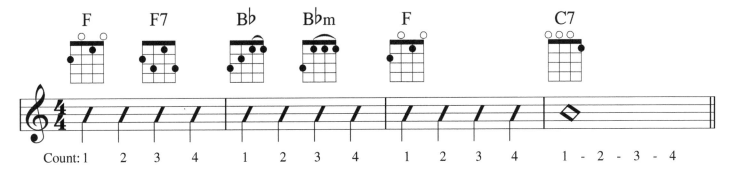

And here's how we make it an ending:

Key of C:

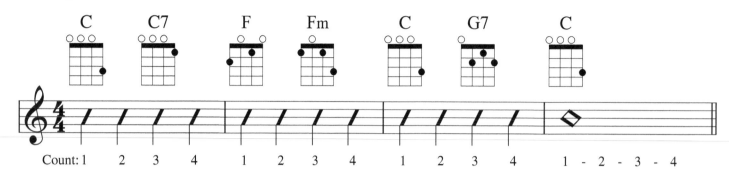

Count: 1   2   3   4   1   2   3   4   1   2   3   4   1 - 2 - 3 - 4

Key of F:

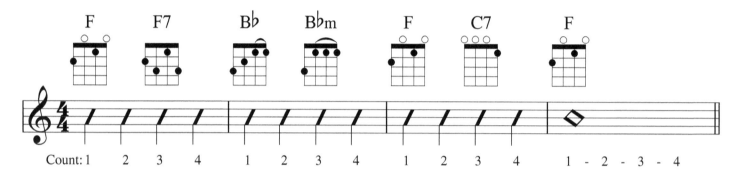

Count: 1   2   3   4   1   2   3   4   1   2   3   4   1 - 2 - 3 - 4

Lil Rev's Golden Rule of Intros and Endings
Often, the difference between an intro and an ending is determined by the last chord in the sequence. If it returns to the I chord, it's an ending; if it adds a V chord (G7 in the key of C, for example) at the end, it's an intro.

THE GUS KAHN INTRO

Gus Kahn was one of the pre-eminent songwriters of the vaudeville, Tin Pan Alley, and Broadway stage. He was revered by everyone from Al Jolson, Jerome Kern, and George Gershwin to Harry Akst, Harry Woods, and Buddy DeSylva.

His list of songs includes dozens of notable hits, from "Making Whoopee" and "I'll See You in My Dreams," to "Dream a Little Dream of Me" and "It Had to Be You." You'd be hard pressed these days to find a ukulele club songbook that doesn't include at least one song from lyricist Gus Kahn.

Since most lead sheets rarely give anything but lyrics and chords, the benefit of collecting notated folios and old sheet music has never been more apparent, and therein lies a beautiful history of intros and endings.

This intro works great on all Tin Pan Alley-type songs like Gus's tune "Dream a Little Dream of Me" or "Making Whoopee." The last chord should be struck once and held for the duration of the measure, counting "2, 3, 4" before launching into your song.

Key of G:

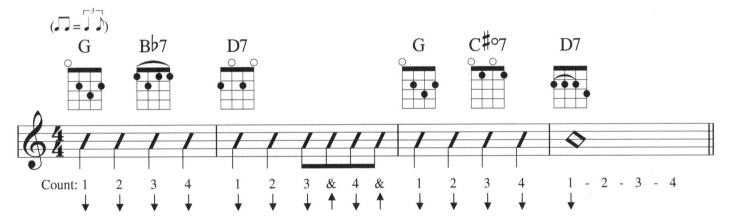

Key of C:

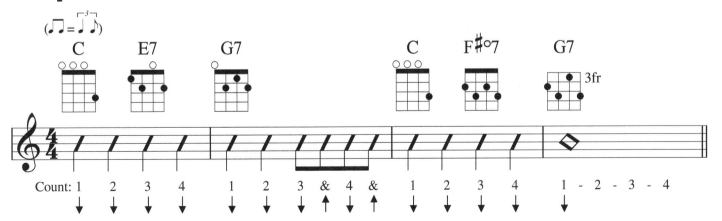

THE TIN PAN ALLEY TURNAROUND

In the summer of 2013, I embarked on a study of some 300 pieces of sheet music I had collected from rummage sales, flea markets, antique malls, and estate sales. The pieces dated from 1890 to 1950.

As I looked at this giant body of song from a bygone era, I asked myself if each decade or generation of writers had used any similar devices in their transitions (or turns) between verses. Much to my surprise, I discovered that a great number of writers (from the '20s and '30s) were all using the same turn.

A *turn* (short for *turnaround*) is a chordal vamp that brings you back to the next verse, much like a Hawaiian vamp starts the song over or a blues turnaround leads into the next verse.

Below is my favorite turnaround in the style of Tin Pan Alley songwriter Buddy DeSylva (who was also an accomplished ukulele player). Buddy wrote an incredible array of songs as well as entire film scores for *The Singing Fool, Sunny Side Up*, and *Just Imagine*. His biggest hit was "Look for the Silver Lining."

You can insert this turn after any verse to steer the listener back into the next, though it's most effective when used with Broadway-type show tunes, comedic, jazz, jug band, novelty, or Tin Pan Alley repertoire.

Given a rest after the V chord, a Tin Pan Alley turn can also be used as an intro.

Key of C:

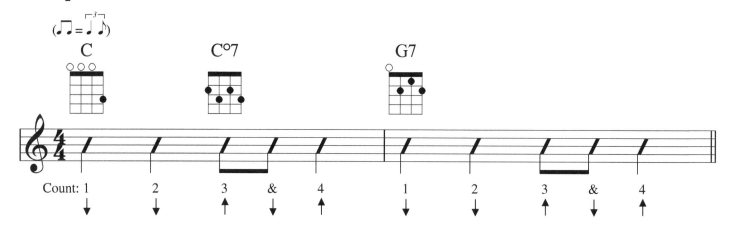

Key of F:

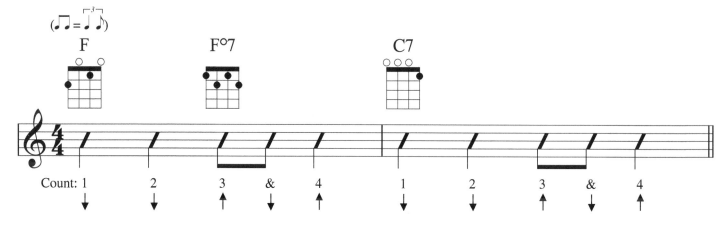

Key of G:

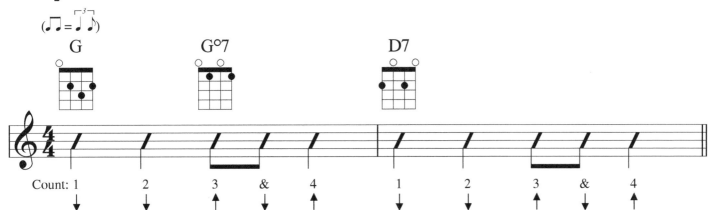

Key of A:

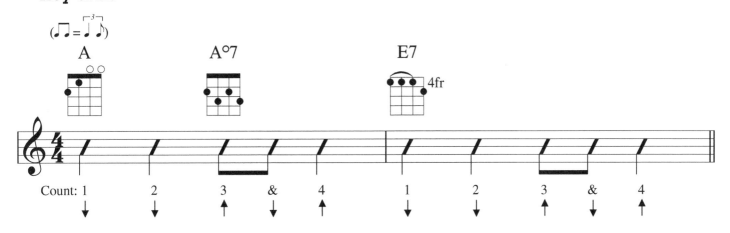

Key of D:

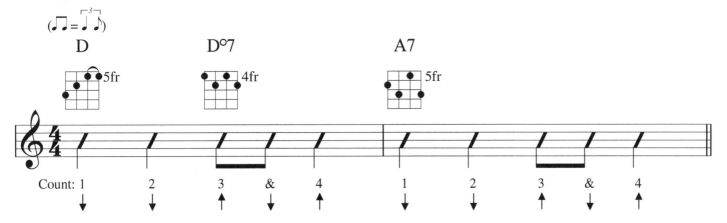

Key of E:

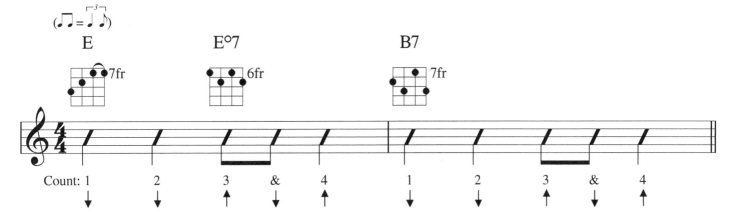

BLUESY ROLL-SLAP WITH TREMOLO-SLIDE ENDING

Bluesy slap endings were used by a wide variety of blues guitar giants like the late Big Bill Broonzy and Scrapper Blackwell, as well as folkies like Dave Van Ronk and Eric Von Schmidt.

Slapping, snapping, tapping, and pulling at the strings, or plucking upwards on chords, was commonplace in the blues idiom, especially amongst artists like Sam Chatmon of the Mississippi Sheiks and Delta bluesmen like Charley Patton and Bukka White. The percussive nature of this kind of playing gives it a real unique flavor and helps to create a highly definitive ending.

This ending is most at home in the blues idiom, but artists like Bob Gibson and other roots-based folkies have often employed this to great effect with folk, bluegrass, jug band, and even country styles.

Follow this procedure to perform this ending:

1. Review roll strokes, tremolo, and chordal tremolo slides at the beginning of the video.

2. Strum each respective chord once, then immediately slap down onto the fretboard across the strings, so that each chord you play has one roll stroke and one slap.

3. Do not strum, but rather *tremolo slide* into the last chord of the sequence. Tremolo is indicated by ⫸ in the music.

Note: It will take a bit of practice to work up all the techniques necessary for this ending, but it's well worth the effort. Be patient and soon applause will follow.

Big Bill Broonzy

Key of E:

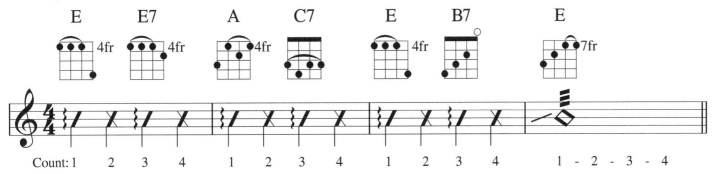

Count: 1   2   3   4   1   2   3   4   1   2   3   4   1 - 2 - 3 - 4

Key of F:

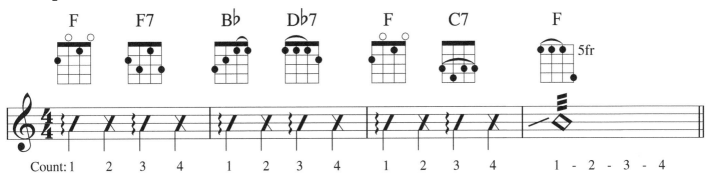

Count: 1   2   3   4   1   2   3   4   1   2   3   4   1 - 2 - 3 - 4

Key of G:

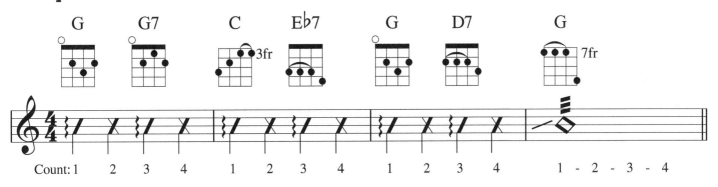

Count: 1   2   3   4   1   2   3   4   1   2   3   4   1 - 2 - 3 - 4

Key of A:

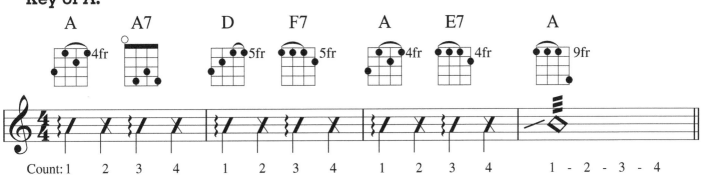

Count: 1   2   3   4   1   2   3   4   1   2   3   4   1 - 2 - 3 - 4

HAWAIIAN VAMPS

My old pal, the late John King, once said that, by 1917, three quarters of the dance hall orchestras in America had at least one or two Tin Pan Alley Hawaiian numbers in their playlist. All things Hawaiian were the craze of the day, and sheet music to "Aloha 'Oe" was selling millions of copies, whilst performers like Al Jolson were singing "Yaaka Hula Hickey Dula" in shows like *Robinson Crusoe, Jr.*

Since those pivotal days, it's become widely accepted that running a ukulele club, holding a ukulele festival, or putting on a good ukulele show without at least a sprinkling of island flavor is akin to buying your ticket and missing the boat! It's safe to say, Hawaiian music is here to stay—a cultural treasure that honors its past while pressing onwards. As you get to know this joyful music, you'll soon discover that nothing is as stylistically definitive as the Hawaiian vamp, which is, by its very nature, both an easy intro and a tried and true turnaround.

Let's look at how this works. If we're in C, for example, we'd start on D7 (II7) for two counts, then move to G7 (V7) for two counts, and finally return to the tonic of C for four counts. Thus, it's a II7–V7–I progression.

In addition to its use as a turnaround, Hawaiian vamps make wonderful intros or outros as well. Following is a list of Hawaiian vamps in seven of the most common keys.

Remember: two counts on the II7 chord, two counts on the V7, and four counts on the I complete the strum cycle of a Hawaiian vamp.

All of the following examples are counted/strummed the same: 1 2 3 4, 1 2 3 & 4.

Key of C:

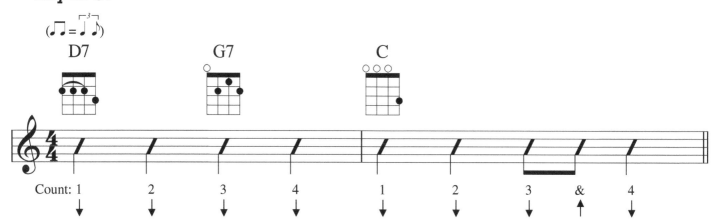

Key of D:

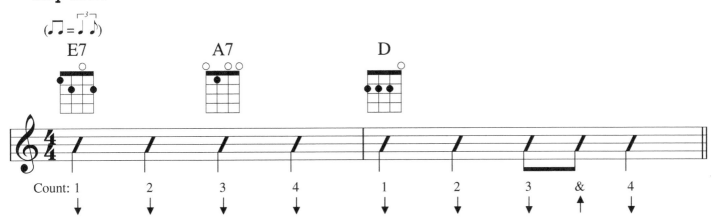

Key of E:

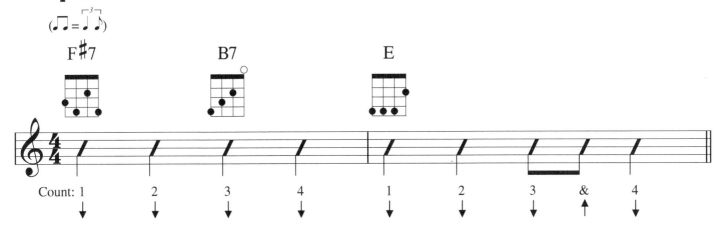

Key of F:

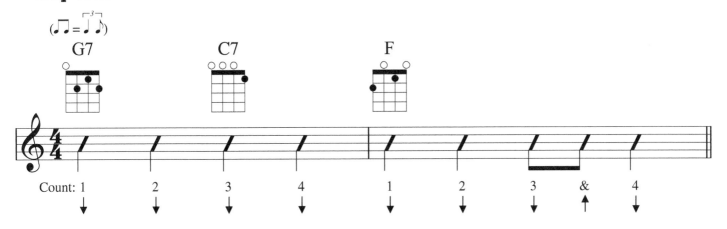

Key of G:

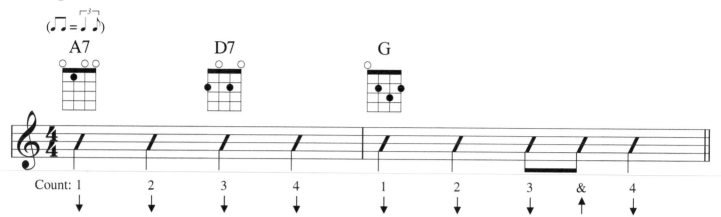

Count: 1   2   3   4   1   2   3   &   4

Key of A:

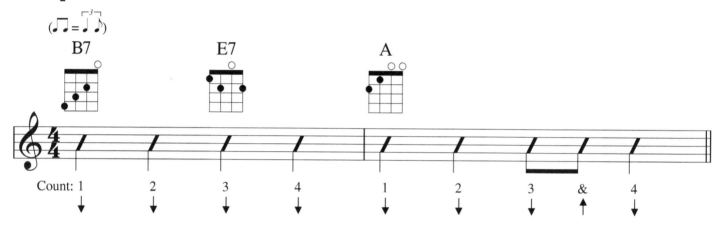

Count: 1   2   3   4   1   2   3   &   4

Key of B♭:

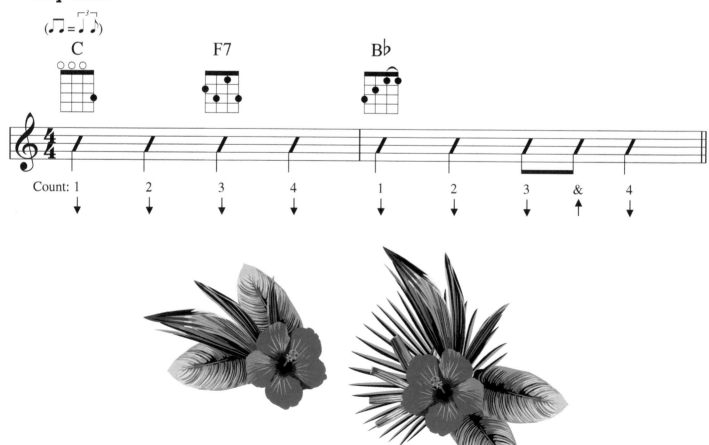

Count: 1   2   3   4   1   2   3   &   4

SHAVE AND A HAIRCUT ENDING

Below you'll find the classic bluegrass ending known as "Shave and a Haircut."

I've transcribed it for five of the most common bluegrass keys.

To apply this simple melodic tag, just staple it onto the very end of a song. Instantly, it spells the end of a tune!

Key of C:

Key of D:

Key of F:

Key of G:

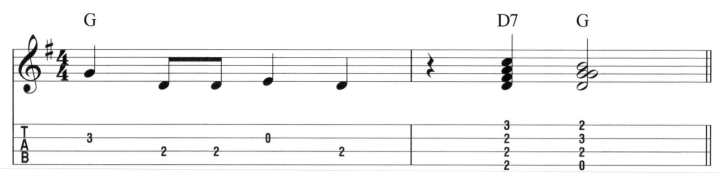

Key of A:

FATTY ARBUCKLE'S BIG START

Roscoe Conkling, aka Fatty Arbuckle (1887–1933), was one of the biggest stars of the teens and '20s, raking in a whopping one million dollars when he signed with Paramount Pictures in 1920. His 14 films with Buster Keaton (who was also a ukulele enthusiast) and his impressive body of shorts and features offer us a magic window into a time and place when entertainers like Fatty got their start young, honing their skills in traveling road shows and theater troupes.

Fatty was so much more than an actor. He was an acrobat, master of sleight of hand, consummate jokester, first-rate singer, and juggler, to name but a few of his many skills. Like many from his era, he flirted with the ukulele as both a prop and as a means for delivering a tune. His larger-than-life size belied his onstage antics, and some, like operatic singer Caruso, went so far as to discourage his comedic acting endeavors in favor of a more palatable profession like a singing career!

The following intro was synonymous with Fatty's heyday from 1911–1925 and was well known by most ukulele-playing stage entertainers as a stock intro.

Strum each chord once, but hold each for a two-count, counting: 1-2, 3-4, 1-2, 3-4, etc.

Key of G:

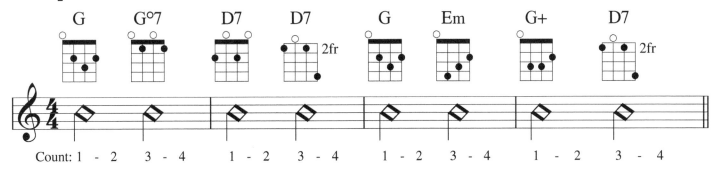

Fatty Arbuckle

STORMY MONDAY INTRO

Jazzy, jump, and shuffle blues were in vogue in the '40s and '50s with the likes of Charles Brown, Big Joe Turner, Johnny Moore, Nat King Cole, Clarence "Gatemouth" Brown, Bill Jennings, and the reigning king, T-Bone Walker. Walker, who was born in Oak Cliff, Texas in 1910 (and died in 1975), had a huge impact on iconic players like Chuck Berry, Jimi Hendrix, and (much later) Stevie Ray Vaughan. His lead style was based on electrified, horn-inspired, single-note lines, and he peppered his shows with theatrical antics—doing the splits while taking a solo or playing behind his head, with his teeth, and between his legs.

The ukulele, with its easily accessible palette of three- and four-fingered jazz chords, makes the study of T-Bone's rhythm style highly manageable. Not only is this a super cool intro to add to your bag of tricks, but it's a great study in playing inverted chord forms up the neck—especially if you aren't already familiar with moveable 9th and 13th chords on the ukulele. Note that these are all rootless voicings, meaning that the C9 chords don't have a C in them, the B♭9 chords don't have a B♭ in them, etc. Nevertheless, the harmonic intent is still clear.

T-Bone regularly used a free-form, two-bar intro to open slower blues tunes like "Mean Old World" and "Stormy Monday." Because these intros were almost always unaccompanied, T-Bone played them very loosely, so watch the video to get a good sense of how this classic intro should be phrased.

Key of C:

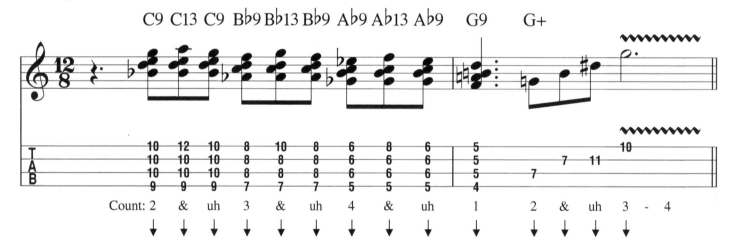

T-Bone Walker

MELODIC TAG ENDINGS

Tag endings have come a long way since their humble beginnings in the early '20s, when country music was still in its infancy. Hotshot string band guitarists like Riley Puckett, Roy Harvey, and Sam McGee all employed catchy little bass runs, chromatic chord connectors, and a wide vocabulary of tag endings often inspired by the fiddlers that they performed with.

Today, country guitar pickers and Nashville session musicians lovingly carry on these traditions—from the well-known "Flatt run" of bluegrass fame to the pyrotechnics of stop-time endings executed by players like Albert Lee, Danny Gatton, or the legendary Hank Garland.

Until recently, the ukulele's dynamic and fascinating rhythmic nature has historically relegated it to a back seat role in country music. Fortunately, today's crop of melodically informed players like Fred Sokolow, Aaron Keim, James Hill, Jake Shimabukuro, and Gerald Ross have inspired us to move way beyond its enticing strum factor.

Below you'll find three, two-bar tag endings notated in three of the most common ukulele keys of C, F, and G. Take the time to play through each slowly, knowing repetition is the key to playing these well in a real jam situation. Once you can play through these cleanly, try increasing the tempo a bit until you are able to tie them onto the end of your favorite bluegrass or country song without falling apart.

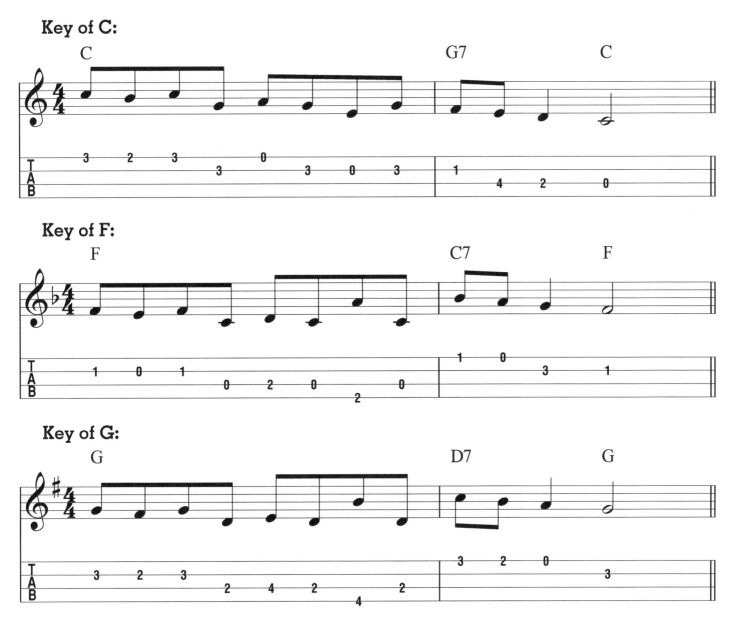

BLUES TURNAROUND VARIATIONS IN A

The *blues turnaround* is a musical phrase that's played over the I and V chords in the last two bars of a blues progression. Its main purpose is to set up the form to repeat, leading its user into the next verse or instrumental passage. The common blues turnaround evolved from humble roots in early jazz and ragtime to become an integral part of the standard 12-bar blues form.

Certainly, one measure of today's professional blues guitarist is rooted in his or her ability to employ a wide variety of blues turnarounds, with an almost infinite number of possibilities available. Because the typical blues turnaround descends in half steps (chromatically) from the ♭7th to the 5th of the tonic (I chord), a great number of blues artists often begin a song with the turnaround as its intro.

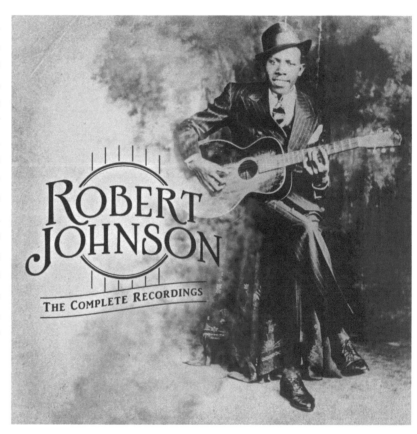

I've given four variations on a blues turnaround theme in A. The first example is in the style of Delta blues legend Robert Johnson and should be plucked using either the first or middle finger and the thumb. For consistency, the first three all share a signature final-measure walkup to the V. The second, third, and fourth are all slight variations on a Chicago blues-style turnaround. The fourth example is a moveable turnaround—i.e., it contains no open strings—that's worth transposing into other keys like F, G, or C.

Variation 1

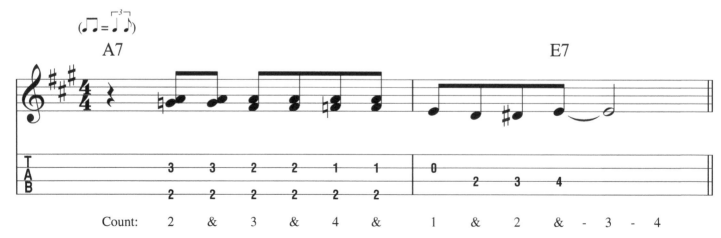

Variation 2

Count: 2   &   uh   3   &   uh   4   &   uh   1   &   2   & - 3 - 4

Variation 3

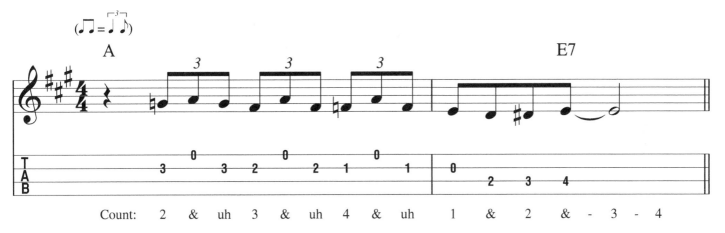

Count: 2   &   uh   3   &   uh   4   &   uh   1   &   2   & - 3 - 4

Variation 4

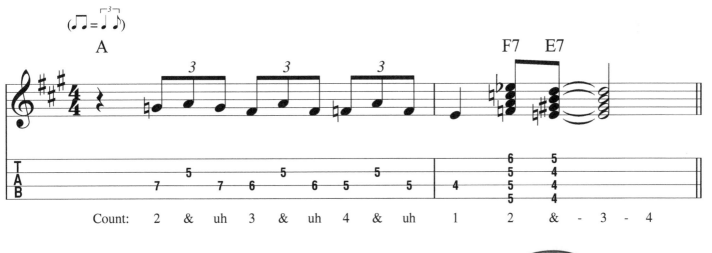

Count: 2   &   uh   3   &   uh   4   &   uh   1   2   & - 3 - 4

THE YIDDISH THEATER INTRO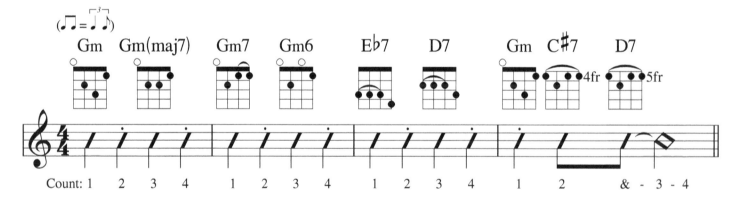

The Yiddish Theater ran parallel to Broadway in the '20s and '30s on the lower east side of Manhattan, as well as many other metropolitan cities across the U.S. where the Jewish population centers could support such endeavors.

Like Broadway, and in some respects vaudeville, the goal of the theater was top-notch drama sprinkled with song and humor—all at an affordable price.

In what is now the East Village, Second Avenue was once home to over a dozen different Yiddish theaters. While these theaters are gone forever, they gave birth to a brilliant body of Yiddish song, ranging from comedic to love ballads.

Steeped in a rich tradition of song and leaning towards the minor side of things, the composers of the Yiddish Theater looked to create intros and endings that matched the brilliance of their Tin Pan Alley comrades, albeit in a minor key.

Here's one of my favorite intros that I've often heard performed with songs like "Bei Mir Bist Du Schein" or "Oy Mayn Kapelye." This could also work well with minor-key classics like Gershwin's "Summer Time" or Berlin's "Blue Skies."

The example below is written in G minor and played in 4/4 with a swing feel. Play each chord with two strokes until you get to the seventh chord form (Gm). Give that chord one staccato stroke before striking C#7 and D7 each one time.

Key of G minor:

Courtesy of Photofest

ROY'S ENDING IN G

Leroy "Roy" Smeck was born February 6th, 1900, in Reading, Pennsylvania. He got his start playing shows on the vaudeville circuit. Working exclusively as an instrumentalist, his presentations showcased virtuosic skills, tricks, flips, taps, blowing into the ukulele, highly melodic picking, and propulsive chord solos. He truly was the first popular ukulele player to gain national recognition in the roaring '20s as anything more than a simple strummer. His skills defied reason and owed as much to his consummate musical abilities as his highly regarded showmanship.

Throughout his storied career, he was often billed as "The Wizard of the Strings," performing on tenor banjo, guitar, lap steel, harmonica, and ukulele. A musician's musician, he carried endorsements from Gibson Guitar Company and Harmony of Chicago. He also designed his own ukulele, the Vita-Uke, which was marketed by Harmony.

To compliment his instrument and record sales, he wrote instructional books and continued to record over the course of multiple decades, eventually recording over 500 sides with companies like Decca, Edison, Victor, Crown, and RCA. His movie shorts made in the '20s are still being viewed and often seen on YouTube, as are his renditions of "Ukulele Tapping," "12th Street Rag," "Tiger Rag," and more.

Below is one of the most beautiful endings I have ever heard. It's spirited after Roy's favored use of diminished chords inverted up the neck, adding 6th, 7th, and 9th chords to round out the flow of this dynamic ending. Use it at the end of any Broadway, Tin Pan Alley, novelty, jug band, or original in the key of G.

Note: As with many of these intros and endings, it should be played with a sense of swing but also *rubato*—i.e., speeding up and/or slowing down with expression.

Key of G:

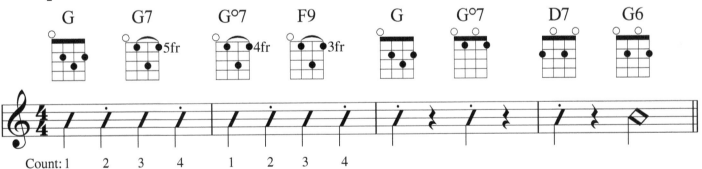

Roy Smeck

MYRON FLOREN'S BIG BAND ENDING

Myron Floren (1919–2005) was highly regarded as one of the greatest accordion players of all time. As a featured star on *The Lawrence Welk Show*, his solos endeared him to a whole generation of music lovers and polka fans. From 1950–1980, Myron continued with the *Welk Show* and his traveling band, never failing to perform his signature piece, "Lady of Spain," to loving fans worldwide.

As a kid, my mom would occasionally let me stay up late if—and only if—I agreed to watch reruns of *The Lawrence Welk Show* with her! I remember being spellbound by Myron's dancing fingers and, for a short while, I even tried my hand at learning to play the accordion. Years later, I began playing in nursing homes, and it was Myron's influence that served me, as I performed "Just Because Polka," "Green, Green Grass of Home," "Malaguena," "Barbara Polka," "You Are My Sunshine," and "When You Wore a Tulip."

This ending takes its influence from groups like Duke Ellington, Count Basie, and Glenn Miller, whose swinging big bands would often end slower numbers with this combination of major, diminished, 6th, 9th, and major 7th chords. Strike each chord once, counting 1-2 for each stroke, and be sure to either let the last chord ring out or finish with tremolo on the final major 7th chord. It really doesn't get any cooler than this one!

BYE BYE BLACKBIRD INTRO

As an audiophile, I first heard "Bye Bye Blackbird" played on an old LP by Nick Lucas and then later Gene Austin—two greats, both of whom got their start in the roaring '20s.

"Bye Bye Blackbird" was first published in 1926 by the prolific songwriting team of Mort Dixon and Ray Henderson. It was part of an era of song that became known as the American Songbook. Stylistically, it was perfect for the era's crooners, like Nick Lucas, Rudy Vallee, Bing Crosby, and (much later) Frank Sinatra.

The example below had become a stock example of a classic intro by the time "Bye Bye Blackbird" came out in 1926. I'm not sure where I first heard it used with the tune, but it's a cool vintage intro that does epitomize the era's use of diminished, major, and minor 7th chord forms.

The five-chord sequence of this intro is elegantly simple, easy to remember, and is one worth knowing in a variety of keys. It works well with jazz, Broadway, jug band, and novelty-type songs.

Play each stroke with a downbeat. Check out the video example and allow the final 7th chord to ring out for counts 3 and 4 before starting your song. Let's try it in six different keys.

Key of F:

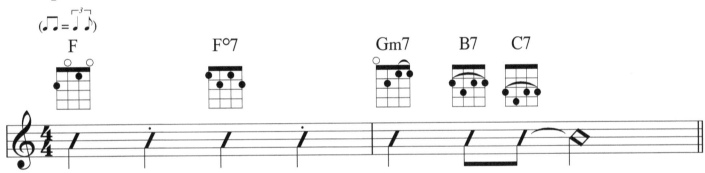

Key of B♭:

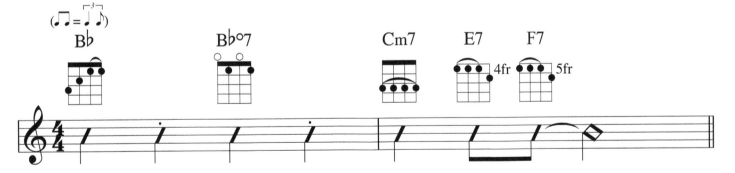

Key of G:

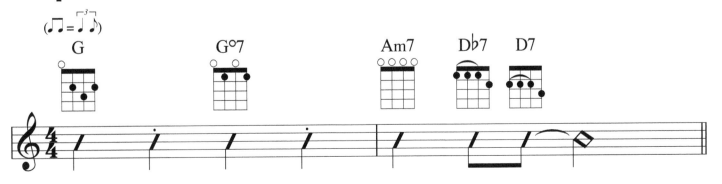

Key of C:

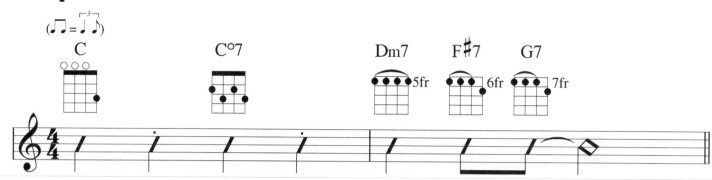

Key of A:

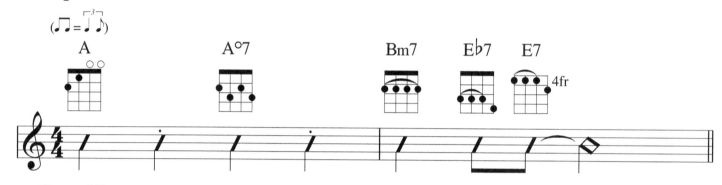

Key of D:

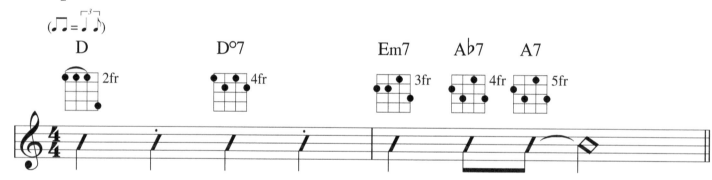

FOUR-NOTE CHROMATIC END LINES

I first discovered the use of chromatic end lines through the work of pioneering country guitarists like Riley Puckett and Sam McGee. Both of these players, and many others of the '20s and '30s, often used simple ascending and/or descending lines that followed the tonic chord and its respective tonal centers of the root, 3rd, and 5th to create interesting chromatic-line endings. This same approach can be accomplished on the ukulele, and even non-melody players will find that plucking four consecutive notes, followed by the tonic chord, is very easy regardless of skill level.

Here's how it works. Once you've finished the last verse or solo, and you've come to the very last measure, attach the chromatic end line followed immediately by the strummed tonic (I) chord. This makes for a real basic, albeit rock-solid, way to end just about any type of song.

Here are some examples in various keys to give you maximum mileage from this concept using a descending line from the 5th to the 3rd. Watch the video to hear my example played with "Hand Me Down My Walking Cane."

Key of A:

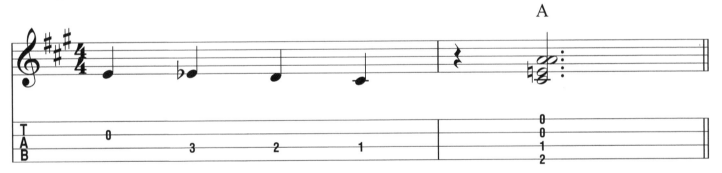

Key of C:

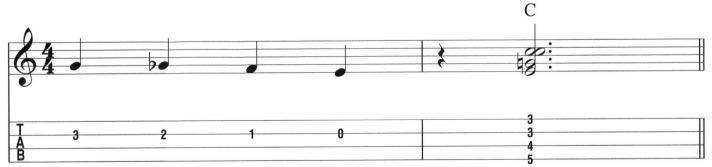

Key of F:

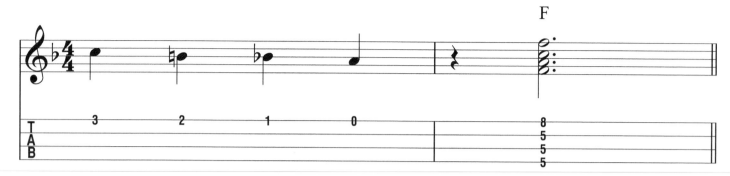

Key of G:

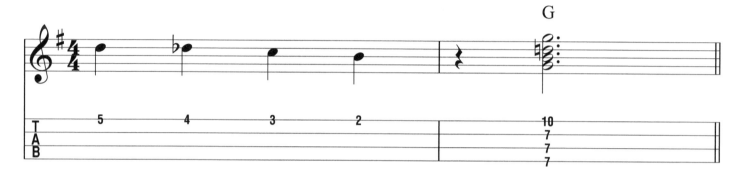

Try This!

For a great effect, let the band fall out while you play the four-note sequence, joining again to strike the last chord together.

BILL TAPIA'S INTRO

Over the years, I've taught and performed with some of the greatest ukulele players in the world. Though many of these giants have long since passed on, their words, stories, and style linger on to guide us as we seek what they sought.

One of the greatest players I had the pleasure of connecting with was the late Bill Tapia, whose birth in 1908 made him one of the precious few remaining links to a bygone era. Performing professionally as young as eight years old, "Tappy"—or "Uncle Bill," as he was called later in life—went on to perform with everyone from Bing Crosby and Louis Armstrong to Elvis Presley.

His performances were always a history lesson in taste, melody, and style. Bill told me once at the New York Ukulele Festival that "the mad rush to play 10,000 notes per solo was the biggest hurdle standing in the way of every up-and-coming young player." His advice was to "slow down, play the melody once or twice, then play around it and finally play the melody one last time; otherwise, everything starts to sound like a scale."

An impeccable dresser, he wore vibrant red-colored suits alongside his signature red ukulele. Bill was also a collector of classic intros and endings. He said that "it was the American Songbook that taught us best—how important it was to have a good intro and ending."

To that effect, here's an intro in the style of Bill Tapia in six different keys.

Key of C:

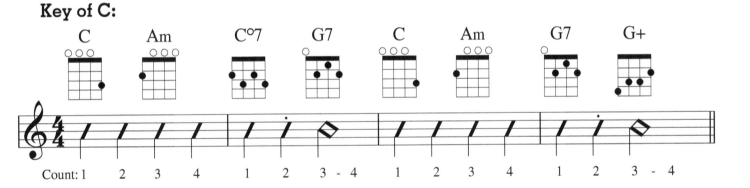

Key of D:

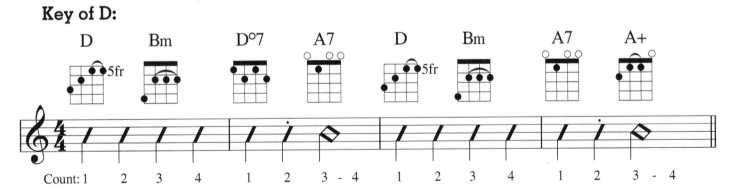

Key of F:

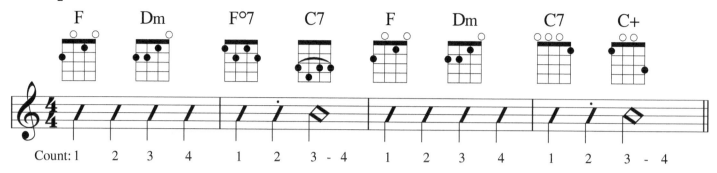

Key of G:

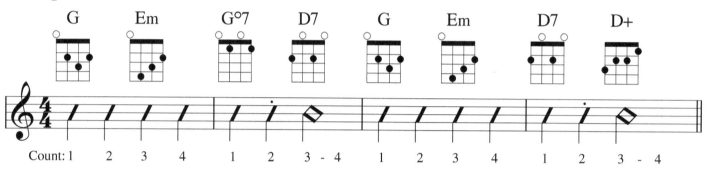

Key of A:

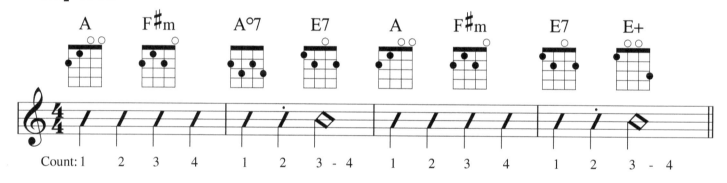

Key of B♭:

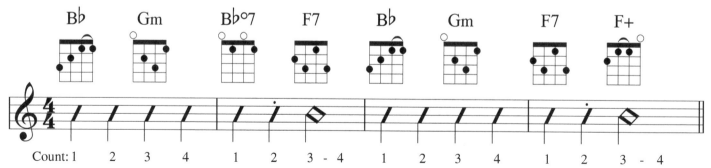

THE REVEREND GARY DAVIS SLIDE ENDING

Reverend Gary Davis was born in Laurens, South Carolina in 1898 into a family of eight children. He took up guitar while in his youth and became a figurehead of the Durham, North Carolina Piedmont blues scene, teaching legendary figures like Blind Boy Fuller. In 1937, just as he became an ordained minister, Davis began to fuse blues, ragtime, and gospel into a flawless two-finger guitar-picking style. His numerous recordings over the years inspired Bob Dylan, the Grateful Dead, the Lovin' Spoonful, Peter, Paul and Mary, Dave Van Ronk, and many others.

While this slide ending is synonymous with Reverend Gary Davis, chances are he first heard this lick played by early country artists. Today it's a stock bluegrass lick all too often credited to Flatt and Scruggs. Davis's approach was to place a rest between the end of a song and his slide ending. His performance style was solo-based, so he played with a great deal of emotional freedom and rubato, slapping the guitar, snapping strings, and slurring or sliding chords and notes at will. The main feature of this lick is to slide into the first note from the root. All in all, it makes a snappy little melodic ending that's highly effective for the solo performer to use as an impressive ending.

Key of F:

Key of G:

Key of A:

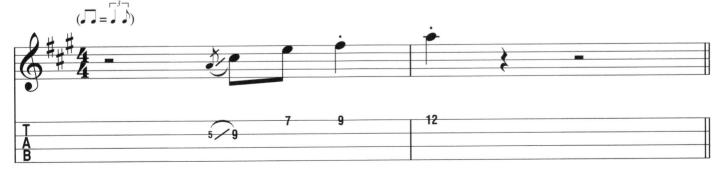

SILVERY MOON INTRO

I first heard "By the Light of the Silvery Moon" sung to me by my mother, who sang it as a bedtime lullaby. The song was written by Gus Edwards and Edward Madden in 1909 and later featured in dozens of television and motion picture shows.

Gus Edwards would later go on to write "In My Merry Oldsmobile" and "School Days," among hundreds of other favorites. The earliest renditions were marketed to piano players who had no problem at all playing sophisticated intros for this kind of sentimental ballad.

It doesn't get much classier than this, so use it as a stand-in intro to any Tin Pan Alley, Broadway, or doo-wop tune.

Below you'll find this intro written out in the keys of A and C.

Key of A:

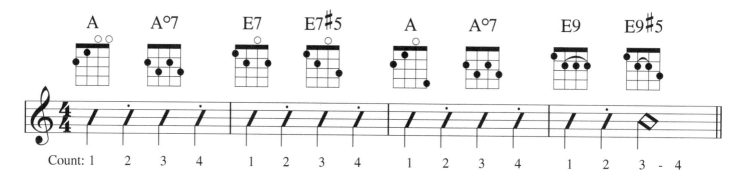

Key of C:

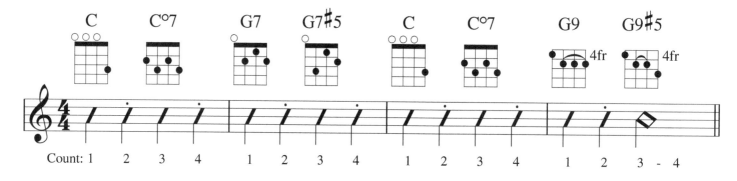

MINOR VAMP INTROS

A *vamp* is a repeating musical figure or, as my pro music pals like to say, "a progression that doesn't go anywhere."

Jazz vamps shouldn't be confused with the Hawaiian vamps, which are used as turnarounds and intros in Hawaiian music. Major- and minor-key vamps, when used in jazz, are played for longer durations of time, often before a tune's *head* (melody or main body) has begun. The intro vamp also provides a sweet spot for instrumentalists to improvise over the front end of a tune.

The list of tunes that these diatonic minor progressions work well with is as infinite as the whole of American popular music, and every jazz musician worth his or her bread and butter knows how to play them in a multitude of different keys.

Rhythmically, they are punchy, fun to play, and can really help set up the groove.

The rule of thumb for the following six intro vamps in 4/4 time is to strum each chord just once in the progression, paying attention to the shift in accent on the second and fourth chords. I play the first and third chords on the downbeat, but the second and fourth chords are on the upbeat. As always, watch and listen to the video example to get a good feel.

Key of A minor:

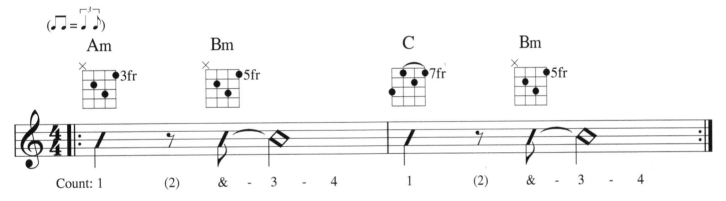

Key of D minor:

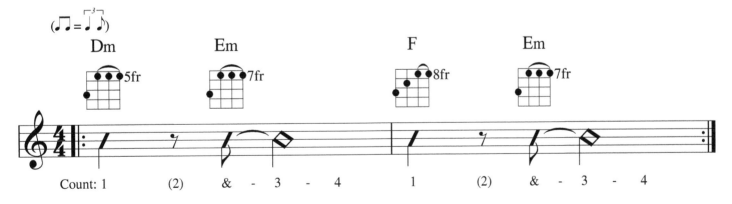

Try This!
Another cool ending trick used by all the pros is to repeat the last four measures of a song melody. Thus, when the song would normally end, one of the lead instruments plays (or repeats) the last four measures of the melody as a *tag ending*.

Key of B♭ minor:

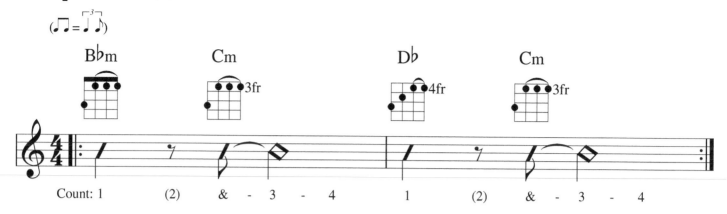

Count: 1   (2)   & - 3 - 4   1   (2)   & - 3 - 4

Key of F minor:

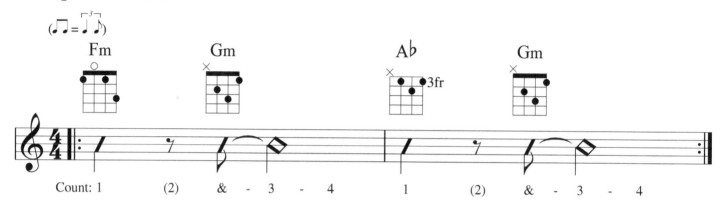

Count: 1   (2)   & - 3 - 4   1   (2)   & - 3 - 4

Key of C minor:

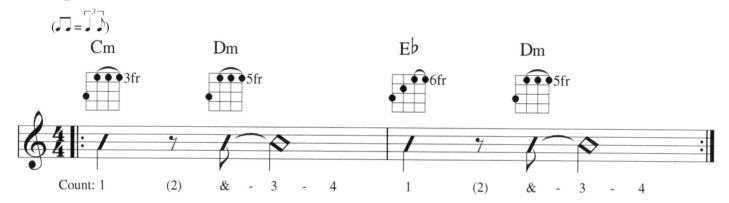

Count: 1   (2)   & - 3 - 4   1   (2)   & - 3 - 4

Key of G minor:

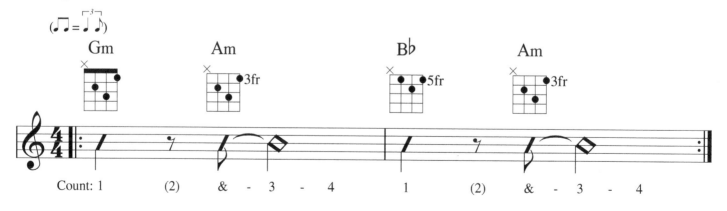

Count: 1   (2)   & - 3 - 4   1   (2)   & - 3 - 4

REVERSE BASIE ENDING

Legendary jazz pianist Count Basie's first piano lessons reputedly cost him 25 cents! He must have been a great student, because his exceptional, blues-infused compositions and extraordinary bandleader skills served him well with a career that spanned over 60 years. From Harlem to Kansas City and later Chicago, Basie coasted on a song from the mid '20s, leading his band right on into the '80s while appearing in movies, television, festivals, cruises, and an endless array of recordings. He infused early jazz with ragtime, blues, swing, bop, rock, and Latin flavors, inspiring countless generations of jazz fans along the way.

He is remembered today for such classics as "One O'Clock Jump" (1937), "Jumpin' at the Woodside" (1939), and "Taxi War Dance" (1939).

Below we'll look at what is commonly called a IVmaj7–#IV°7–V7–I progression, which is used by jazz-heads from coast to coast.

For example, in the following keys, this progression would be as follows:

- **Key of C:** Fmaj7–F#°7–G7–C

- **Key of F:** B♭maj7–B°7–C7–F

- **Key of G:** Cmaj7–C#°7–D7–G

- **Key of A:** Dmaj7–D#°7–E7–A

I have heard everyone from Australia's great Azo Bell to the Mainland's Lyle Ritz, Bill Tapia, and Curt Sheller use this ending to great effect. What has always fascinated me most about this ending, however, is that it sounds 100 times better when played in reverse! This is often called a *reverse Basie ending*.

Here is the reverse Basie ending written out in the popular ukulele key of C.

Key of C:

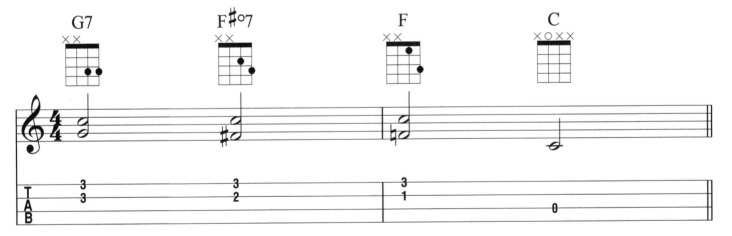

Try This!

Another neat trick: instead of plucking the open C as the last note, play the C as a 12th-fret harmonic. Lightly touch string 3 directly over fret 12 (over the fret wire) with your ring finger without pressing down, pluck the string, and immediately pull your fret-hand ring finger away. The result should be a chiming sound.

PEE WEE CRAYTON'S WEST COAST TURNAROUND

Like the great blues guitarist T-Bone Walker and others of his generation, Pee Wee Crayton left Texas during the war years for California, relocating to Oakland and then later Los Angeles. Recording in 1948 for Jules Bihari's Modern Records, his slow blues groove "Blues After Hours" went to #1 on the R&B charts that very same year. Pee Wee's success was owed as much to his handsome looks as his combined use of piano, saxophone, drums, and guitar. A protégé of T-Bone Walker, Pee Wee rode a wave of popularity straight on through to the mid-'50s and the start of rock 'n' roll.

In the spirit of Pee Wee Crayton, the following example is reminiscent of the kind of blues turnaround used in Pee Wee's "Blues After Hours." It has a swinging uptown sort of feel that makes it great for jazzier, slow tempo blues.

I've written it out in four common ukulele keys.

Key of G:

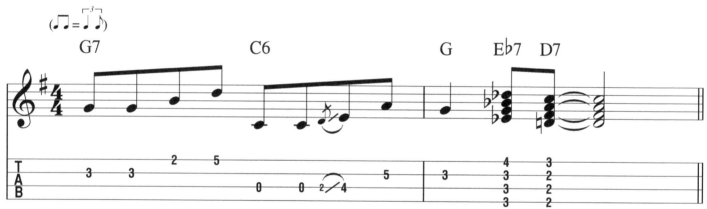

Key of A:

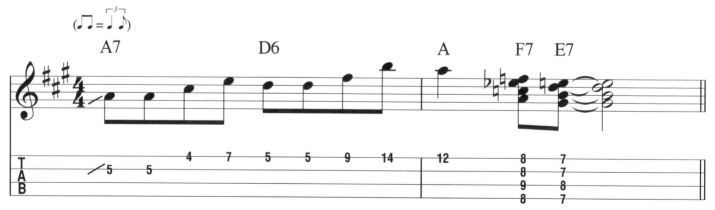

Key of F:

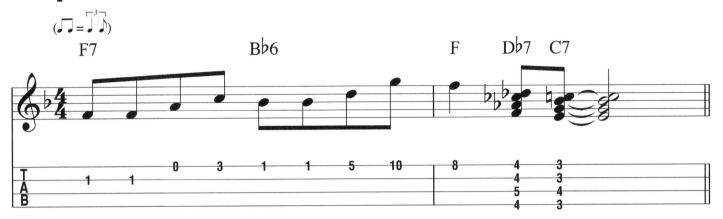

Key of C:

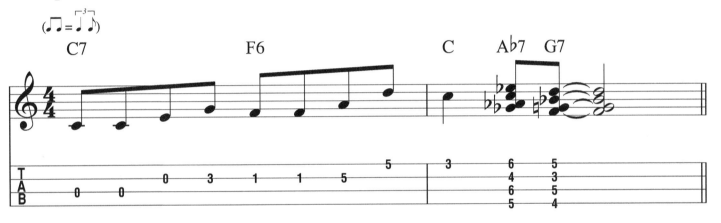

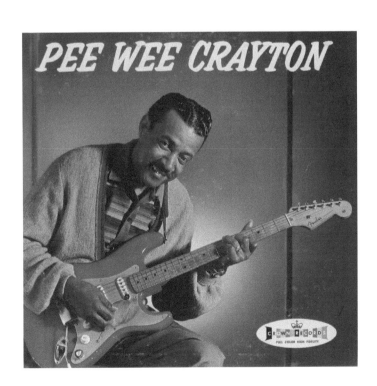

PEE WEE CRAYTON

THE BIRTH OF THE BLUES ENDING

No two genres have given more to the body of intros and endings than early jazz and blues. The study of blues intros alone could fill an encyclopedia of examples.

Some of my favorite intros and endings come from a time when recorded blues was in its infancy, and the great female queens like Ida Cox, Bessie Smith, Alberta Hunter, Ma Rainey, and Mamie Smith where supported by jazz-inspired quintets like Louis Armstrong's Hot Five. This lyrical fusion of jazz and blues, just as the recording industry was discovering its potential, made for some of the most fascinating repertoire.

Do yourself a favor and listen to these early classics:

- "Crazy Blues" (1920): Mamie Smith

- "Gulf Coast Blues" (1923): Bessie Smith

- "Downhearted Blues" (1923): Bessie Smith

- "Sweet Petunia" (1927): Lucille Bogan

- "Organ Grinder Blues" (1928): Victoria Spivey

- "Nobody Knows You When You're Down and Out" (1929): Bessie Smith

- "You Can't Tell the Difference After Dark" (1935): Alberta Hunter

- "Get 'Em from the Peanut Man (Hot Nuts)" (1936): Lil Johnson

Also, listen to Trixie Smith, Sippie Wallace, Bessie Tucker, and Lil Green.

Below we'll look at a classic blues era ending. It's simple, understated, and elegant in its harmonic nature. More than anything, it makes a really beautiful way to end a blues or Tin Pan Alley song. Play this with a slow swing feel using all downbeats.

Key of B♭:

| B♭ | B♭7 | E°7 | E♭m6 | B♭ |

Count: 1   2   3   4   1   2   3   4   1 - 2 - 3 - 4

Key of C:

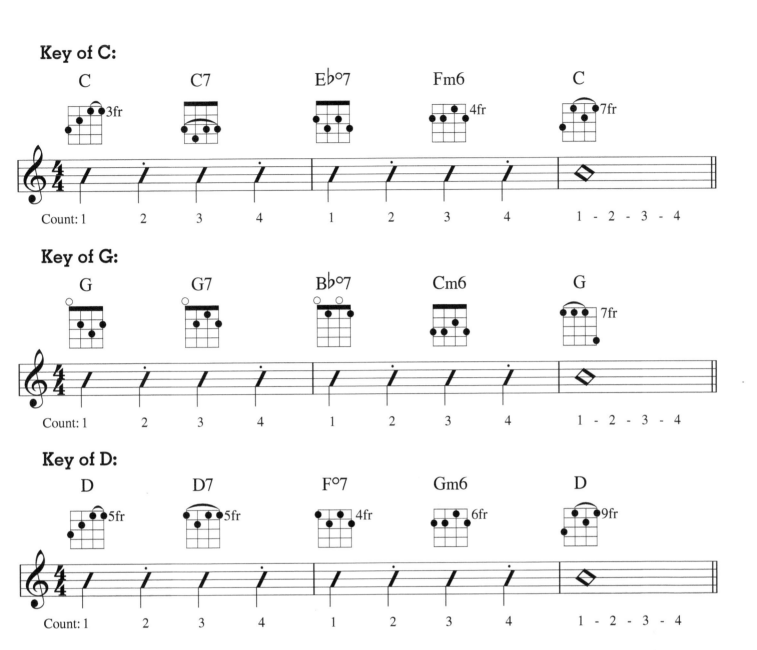

Note: Feel free to tack tremolo onto the last chord for a nice finish!

Bessie Smith

BILL HALEY'S COMET ENDING

Bill Haley was born in Highland Park, Michigan on July 6, 1925. He began playing guitar at 13, and by 18 had recorded his first record called "Candy Kisses." In 1949, his single "Rock This Joint," which is often cited as the first rockabilly record, sold over 75,000 copies and set the stage for more of Haley's unique fusion of blues, country, and rock.

His biggest hit, "Rock Around the Clock," released in 1954 on the Decca Record Label, was not the first rock 'n' roll song to be recorded, though it was the first one to reach the top of the Billboard pop charts. A slow starter, the tune burned up the charts shortly after being used in the opening credits to the 1955 youth culture film *Blackboard Jungle*.

The song was originally written by Max C. Freedman and James E. Meyers in 1952, with its most popular version attributed to Bill Haley and the Comets.

The Guinness Book of World Records lists it as the best-selling rock 'n' roll vinyl single. To date, it has sold more copies than any other pop record short of Bing Crosby's "White Christmas," and estimates to date put it at 25 million copies. Music historians are fancy to note that "Rock Around the Clock" is playing somewhere around the world almost every minute of the day!

The song's intro—"1-2-3-o'clock, 4 o'clock rock"—is one of the most distinctive intros in rock and roll. Far more memorable, though, is the descending scale run that Danny Cedrone played at the session to close out the tune. Below you'll find a simplified variation of the original "Rock Around the Clock" ending. It can be used to end any rock and roll song in A.

Try This!

A good way to get the phrasing right on this ending is to say the word "telephone," broken into three syllables ("tel-e-phone"), for each of the first four phrases.

Key of A:

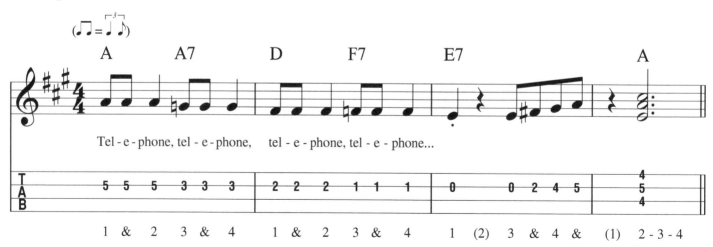

SONG GUIDE FOR INTROS, ENDINGS, AND TURNAROUNDS

Here's a list of fun songs you can use to try out your intros, endings, turnarounds, and vamps. Many of these can be found on YouTube or in Jumpin' Jim's *Daily Ukulele* songbooks, published by Hal Leonard.

Lil' Rev Intro: "In the Still of the Night," "Stand by Me," "Sh-Boom," "Since I Met You Baby," "Abilene"

Lil' Rev Ending: "Have I Told You Lately That I Love you," "Where Have All the Flowers Gone?," "Under the Boardwalk," "Whole Lotta Shakin' Goin' On," "Hound Dog," "My Blue Heaven"

The Gus Kahn Intro: "Ukulele Lady," "I'll See You in My Dreams," "Dream a Little Dream of Me," "Sweet Lorraine," "Do You Know What It Means to Miss New Orleans," "Dinah," "Bewitched," "April Showers"

The Tin Pan Alley Turnaround: "Boodle Am Shake," "Crazy Words," "Crazy Tune," "Where Did Robinson Crusoe Go," "Java Jive," "Blues My Naughty Sweetie Gives to Me," "Lazy Bones"

Blues Roll-Slap with Tremolo-Slide Ending: "St. Louis Blues," "Kansas City Blues," "Stagolee," "Frankie and Johnny," "Hound Dog," "Nobody Knows You When You're Down and Out," "Blues Stay Away from Me," "Drifting Blues," "Ice Cream Man Blues," "In the Evening When the Sun Goes Down Blues"

Hawaiian Vamps: "Hi'ilawe," "Waikiki," "Ku'u Home o Kahalu'u," "Kaulana nã Pua," "Morning Dew," "Pua 'Ãhihi," "Pua Hone," "Amapola," "Akaka Falls," "Kãwika," "Mele Kalikimaka," "Lovely Hula Hands"

Shave and a Haircut Ending: "Rolling in My Sweet Baby's Arms," "Hand Me Down My Walking Cane," "Tom Dooley," "Rocky Top," "Rocky Raccoon," "Sweet Georgia Brown," "Jambalaya," "Darktown Strutters' Ball," "Oh! Susanna"

Fatty Arbuckle's Big Start: "Baby Face," "Always," "I'm Always Chasing Rainbows," "I'm Beginning to See the Light," "For Me and My Gal," "Side by Side," "Sentimental Journey," "On the Beach at Waikiki"

Stormy Monday Intro: "Mean Old World Blues," "Call It Stormy Monday," "Reconsider Baby," "Send Me Someone to Love," "Red House Blues," "Drifting Blues," "Change It," "When It Rains It Pours"

Melodic Tag Endings: "Hey, Good Lookin'," "Act Naturally," "I'm a Believer," "On the Road Again"

Blues Turnaround Variations in A: "Sweet Home Chicago," "Crosscut Saw," "Don't Start Me Talkin'," "Nine Below Zero," "Long Distance Call," "I Got My Mojo Working," "Your Funeral and My Trial"

The Yiddish Theater Intro: "Bei Mir Bist Du Schein," "Blue Skies," "Summertime," "Brother, Can You Spare a Dime?"

Roy's Ending in G: "You're Nobody till Somebody Loves You," "My Funny Valentine," "Limehouse Blues," "Some of These Days," "Let Me Call You Sweetheart," "It's Only a Paper Moon," "Don't Get Around Much Anymore"

Myron Floren's Big Band Ending: "I Can't Give You Anything but Love, Baby," "Georgia," "Beautiful Dreamer," "Ain't Misbehavin'," "Between the Devil and the Deep Blue Sea," "Bewitched"

Bye Bye Blackbird Intro: "All of Me," "For All We Know," "Avalon," "Dinah," "Cuban Pete," "Cecilia"

Four-Note Chromatic End Lines: "Travelin' Man," "Mr. Bojangles," "Blue Moon of Kentucky," "Jamaica Farewell," "Waterloo," "Slow Poke," "Route 66," "Keep on the Sunny Side," "Mr. Tambourine Man"

Bill Tapia's Intro: "Exactly Like You," "Don't Fence Me In," "Don't Blame Me," "In Apple Blossom Time," "It's Been a Long, Long Time," "It's a Sin to Tell a Lie," "Oh, Lady Be Good!," "That's My Desire"

The Reverend Gary Davis Slide Ending: "If I Had My Way," "Samson and Delilah," "12th Street Rag," "Twelve Gates to the City," "I Am in the Band," "Cincinnati Flow Rag," "Candy Man Blues"

Silvery Moon Intro: "Avalon," "As Time Goes By," "Together," "The Birth of the Blues," "Blue Moon"

Minor Vamp Intros: "Summertime," "Blue Skies," "Autumn Leaves," "In a Sentimental Mood"

Reverse Basie Ending: "Blues in the Night," "Stormy Weather," "Embraceable You," "St. Louis Blues," "Banjo Ikey's Old Time Blues," "Sometimes I Think I Love You," "Romance in the Dark"

Pee Wee Crayton's West Coast Turnaround: "Mother Earth Blues," "99," "Fattening Frogs for Snakes," "Love Is Just a Gamble," "I Want a Little Girl," "I'm Still in Love with You," "Bobby Sox Blues"

The Birth of the Blues Ending: "Crazy Blues," "Mean Old Bed Bug Blues," "Ain't Nobody's Business," "After You've Gone," "Careless Love," "Downhearted Blues," "Take Me for a Buggy Ride," "Yonder Come the Blues"

Bill Haley's Comet Ending: "Whole Lotta Shakin' Goin' On," "Hanky Panky," "Mustang Sally," "Jailhouse Rock," "Hi-Heel Sneakers," "Good Vibrations," "Get Rhythm"

ABOUT THE AUTHOR

Photo by Craig Chee

Lil' Rev is an award-winning, multi-instrumentalist story-teller and entertainer from Sheboygan, Wisconsin.

He tours North America as a traveling clinician presenting workshops, concerts, and one-man shows on quilting, Yiddish, ukulele history, Tin Pan Alley, and Jewish folklore.

"Listen to this! Lil' Rev is great!" – Pete Seeger

He can be found at: **www.lilrev.com**

HAL·LEONARD®
UKULELE PLAY-ALONG

1. POP HITS
00701451 Book/CD Pack $15.99

3. HAWAIIAN FAVORITES
00701453 Book/Online Audio $14.99

4. CHILDREN'S SONGS
00701454 Book/Online Audio $14.99

5. CHRISTMAS SONGS
00701696 Book/CD Pack $12.99

6. LENNON & MCCARTNEY
00701723 Book/Online Audio $12.99

7. DISNEY FAVORITES
00701724 Book/Online Audio $14.99

8. CHART HITS
00701745 Book/CD Pack $15.99

9. THE SOUND OF MUSIC
00701784 Book/CD Pack $14.99

10. MOTOWN
00701964 Book/CD Pack $12.99

11. CHRISTMAS STRUMMING
00702458 Book/Online Audio $12.99

12. BLUEGRASS FAVORITES
00702584 Book/CD Pack $12.99

13. UKULELE SONGS
00702599 Book/CD Pack $12.99

14. JOHNNY CASH
00702615 Book/Online Audio $15.99

15. COUNTRY CLASSICS
00702834 Book/CD Pack $12.99

16. STANDARDS
00702835 Book/CD Pack $12.99

17. POP STANDARDS
00702836 Book/CD Pack $12.99

18. IRISH SONGS
00703086 Book/Online Audio $12.99

19. BLUES STANDARDS
00703087 Book/CD Pack $12.99

20. FOLK POP ROCK
00703088 Book/CD Pack $12.99

21. HAWAIIAN CLASSICS
00703097 Book/CD Pack $12.99

22. ISLAND SONGS
00703098 Book/CD Pack $12.99

23. TAYLOR SWIFT
00221966 Book/Online Audio $16.99

24. WINTER WONDERLAND
00101871 Book/CD Pack $12.99

25. GREEN DAY
00110398 Book/CD Pack $14.99

26. BOB MARLEY
00110399 Book/Online Audio $14.99

27. TIN PAN ALLEY
00116358 Book/CD Pack $12.99

28. STEVIE WONDER
00116736 Book/CD Pack $14.99

29. OVER THE RAINBOW & OTHER FAVORITES
00117076 Book/Online Audio $15.99

30. ACOUSTIC SONGS
00122336 Book/CD Pack $14.99

31. JASON MRAZ
00124166 Book/CD Pack $14.99

32. TOP DOWNLOADS
00127507 Book/CD Pack $14.99

33. CLASSICAL THEMES
00127892 Book/Online Audio $14.99

34. CHRISTMAS HITS
00128602 Book/CD Pack $14.99

35. SONGS FOR BEGINNERS
00129009 Book/Online Audio $14.99

36. ELVIS PRESLEY HAWAII
00138199 Book/Online Audio $14.99

37. LATIN
00141191 Book/Online Audio $14.99

38. JAZZ
00141192 Book/Online Audio $14.99

39. GYPSY JAZZ
00146559 Book/Online Audio $15.99

40. TODAY'S HITS
00160845 Book/Online Audio $14.99

HAL·LEONARD®
www.halleonard.com

Prices, contents, and availability subject to change without notice.

The Best Songs Ever

70 songs have now been arranged for ukulele. Includes: Always • Bohemian Rhapsody • Memory • My Favorite Things • Over the Rainbow • Piano Man • What a Wonderful World • Yesterday • You Raise Me Up • and more.
00282413........$17.99

Campfire Songs for Ukulele

30 favorites to sing as you roast marshmallows and strum your uke around the campfire. Includes: God Bless the U.S.A. • Hallelujah • The House of the Rising Sun • I Walk the Line • Puff the Magic Dragon • Wagon Wheel • You Are My Sunshine • and more.
00129170 ....$14.99

The Daily Ukulele

arr. Liz and Jim Beloff
Strum a different song everyday with easy arrangements of 365 of your favorite songs in one big songbook! Includes favorites by the Beatles, Beach Boys, and Bob Dylan, folk songs, pop songs, kids' songs, Christmas carols, and Broadway and Hollywood tunes, all with a spiral binding for ease of use.
00240356 Original Edition.........$39.99
00240681 Leap Year Edition $39.99
00119270 Portable Edition $37.50

Disney Hits for Ukulele

Play 23 of your favorite Disney songs on your ukulele. Includes: The Bare Necessities • Cruella De Vil • Do You Want to Build a Snowman? • Kiss the Girl • Lava • Let It Go • Once upon a Dream • A Whole New World • and more.
00151250 ....$16.99

Also available:
00291547 **Disney Fun Songs for Ukulele** ...$16.99
00701708 **Disney Songs for Ukulele**.......$14.99
00334696 **First 50 Disney Songs on Ukulele** .$16.99

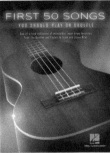

First 50 Songs You Should Play on Ukulele

An amazing collec-tion of 50 accessible, must-know favorites: Edelweiss • Hey, Soul Sister • I Walk the Line • I'm Yours • Imagine • Over the Rainbow • Peaceful Easy Feeling • The Rainbow Connection • Riptide • more.
00149250 ....$16.99
Also available:
00292082 **First 50 Melodies on Ukulele** ...$15.99
00289029 **First 50 Songs on Solo Ukulele**..$15.99
00347437 **First 50 Songs to Strum on Uke** .$16.99

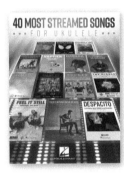

40 Most Streamed Songs for Ukulele

40 top hits that sound great on uke! Includes: Despacito • Feel It Still • Girls like You • Happier • Havana • High Hopes • The Middle • Perfect • 7 Rings • Shallow • Shape of You • Something Just like This • Stay • Sucker • Sunflower • Sweet but Psycho • Thank U, Next • There's Nothing Holdin' Me Back • Without Me • and more!
00298113...........................$17.99

The 4 Chord Songbook

With just 4 chords, you can play 50 hot songs on your ukulele! Songs include: Brown Eyed Girl • Do Wah Diddy Diddy • Hey Ya! • Ho Hey • Jessie's Girl • Let It Be • One Love • Stand by Me • Toes • With or Without You • and many more.
00142050.......$16.99

Also available:
00141143 **The 3-Chord Songbook**........$16.99

Pop Songs for Kids

30 easy pop favorites for kids to play on uke, including: Brave • Can't Stop the Feeling! • Feel It Still • Fight Song • Happy • Havana • House of Gold • How Far I'll Go • Let It Go • Remember Me (Ernesto de la Cruz) • Rewrite the Stars • Roar • Shake It Off • Story of My Life • What Makes You Beautiful • and more.
00284415...........................$16.99

Simple Songs for Ukulele

50 favorites for standard G-C-E-A ukulele tuning, including: All Along the Watchtower • Can't Help Falling in Love • Don't Worry, Be Happy • Ho Hey • I'm Yours • King of the Road • Sweet Home Alabama • You Are My Sunshine • and more.
00156815........$14.99

Also available:
00276644 **More Simple Songs for Ukulele** .$14.99

Top Hits of 2020

18 uke-friendly tunes of 2020 are featured in this collection of melody, lyric and chord arrangements in standard G-C-E-A tuning. Includes: Adore You (Harry Styles) • Before You Go (Lewis Capaldi) • Cardigan (Taylor Swift) • Daisies (Katy Perry) • I Dare You (Kelly Clarkson) • Level of Concern (twenty one pilots) • No Time to Die (Billie Eilish) • Rain on Me (Lady Gaga feat. Ariana Grande) • Say So (Doja Cat) • and more.
00355553...........................$14.99
Also available:
00302274 **Top Hits of 2019** $14.99

Ukulele: The Most Requested Songs

Strum & Sing Series
Cherry Lane Music
Nearly 50 favorites all expertly arranged for ukulele! Includes: Bubbly • Build Me Up, Buttercup • Cecilia • Georgia on My Mind • Kokomo • L-O-V-E • Your Body Is a Wonderland • and more.
02501453...........................$14.99

The Ultimate Ukulele Fake Book

Uke enthusiasts will love this giant, spiral-bound collection of over 400 songs for uke! Includes: Crazy • Dancing Queen • Downtown • Fields of Gold • Happy • Hey Jude • 7 Years • Summertime • Thinking Out Loud • Thriller • Wagon Wheel • and more.
00175500 9" x 12" Edition $45.00
00319997 5.5" x 8.5" Edition $39.99

HAL•LEONARD®

Order today from your favorite music retailer at
halleonard.com

Prices, contents and availability subject to change without notice

Disney characters and artwork TM & © 2021 Disney

UKULELE ENSEMBLE SERIES

The songs in these collections are playable by any combination of ukuleles (soprano, concert, tenor or baritone). Each arrangement features the melody, a harmony part, and a "bass" line. Chord symbols are also provided if you wish to add a rhythm part. For groups with more than three or four ukuleles, the parts may be doubled.

THE BEATLES
Mid-Intermediate Level

All My Loving • Blackbird • Can't Buy Me Love • Eight Days a Week • Here, There and Everywhere • I Want to Hold Your Hand • Let It Be • Love Me Do • Norwegian Wood (This Bird Has Flown) • Penny Lane • Something • Ticket to Ride • When I'm Sixty-Four • Yellow Submarine • Yesterday.
00295927 .... $9.99

CHRISTMAS SONGS
Early Intermediate Level

The Chipmunk Song • The Christmas Song (Chestnuts Roasting on an Open Fire) • Do You Hear What I Hear • Feliz Navidad • Frosty the Snow Man • Have Yourself a Merry Little Christmas • Here Comes Santa Claus (Right Down Santa Claus Lane) • A Holly Jolly Christmas • (There's No Place Like) Home for the Holidays • Jingle Bell Rock • The Little Drummer Boy • Merry Christmas, Darling • The Most Wonderful Time of the Year • Silver Bells • White Christmas.
00129247 .... $9.99

CLASSIC ROCK
Mid-Intermediate Level

Aqualung • Behind Blue Eyes • Born to Be Wild • Crazy Train • Fly Like an Eagle • Free Bird • Hey Jude • Low Rider • Moondance • Oye Como Va • Proud Mary • (I Can't Get No) Satisfaction • Smoke on the Water • Summertime Blues • Sunshine of Your Love.
00103904 .... $10.99

DISNEY FAVORITES
Early Intermediate Level

The Bare Necessities • Beauty and the Beast • Can You Feel the Love Tonight • Colors of the Wind • A Dream Is a Wish Your Heart Makes • It's a Small World • Let It Go • Let's Go Fly a Kite • Little April Shower • Mickey Mouse March • Seize the Day • The Siamese Cat Song • Supercalifragilisticexpialidocious • Under the Sea • A Whole New World.
00279513 .... $9.99

HAWAIIAN SONGS
Mid-Intermediate Level

Aloha Oe • Beyond the Rainbow • Harbor Lights • Hawaiian War Chant (Ta-Hu-Wa-Hu-Wai) • The Hawaiian Wedding Song (Ke Kali Nei Au) • Ka-lu-a • Lovely Hula Hands • Mele Kalikimaka • The Moon of Manakoora • One Paddle, Two Paddle • Pearly Shells (Pupu 'O 'Ewa) • Red Sails in the Sunset • Sleepy Lagoon • Song of the Islands • Tiny Bubbles.
00119254 .... $9.99

THE NUTCRACKER
Late Intermediate Level

Arabian Dance ("Coffee") • Chinese Dance ("Tea") • Dance of the Reed-Flutes • Dance of the Sugar Plum Fairy • March • Overture • Russian Dance ("Trepak") • Waltz of the Flowers.
00119908 .... $9.99

ROCK INSTRUMENTALS
Late Intermediate Level

Beck's Bolero • Cissy Strut • Europa (Earth's Cry Heaven's Smile) • Frankenstein • Green Onions • Jessica • Misirlou • Perfidia • Pick Up the Pieces • Pipeline • Rebel 'Rouser • Sleepwalk • Tequila • Walk Don't Run • Wipe Out.
00103909 .... $9.99

STANDARDS & GEMS
Mid-Intermediate Level

Autumn Leaves • Cheek to Cheek • Easy to Love • Fly Me to the Moon • I Only Have Eyes for You • It Had to Be You • Laura • Mack the Knife • My Funny Valentine • Theme from "New York, New York" • Over the Rainbow • Satin Doll • Some Day My Prince Will Come • Summertime • The Way You Look Tonight.
00103898 .... $9.99

THEME MUSIC
Mid-Intermediate Level

Batman Theme • Theme from E.T. (The Extra-Terrestrial) • Forrest Gump – Main Title (Feather Theme) • The Godfather (Love Theme) • Hawaii Five-O Theme • He's a Pirate • Linus and Lucy • Mission: Impossible Theme • Peter Gunn • The Pink Panther • Raiders March • (Ghost) Riders in the Sky (A Cowboy Legend) • Theme from Spider Man • Theme from "Star Trek®" • Theme from "Superman."
00103903 .... $10.99

www.halleonard.com